Rotherham Library & Information Services

page 2

page 12

This book must be returned by the date specified at the time of issue as
the DUE DATE FOR RETURN.
The loan may be extended (personally, by post, telephone or online) for
a further period, if the book is not required by another reader, by quot-
ing the barcode / author / title.

Enquiries: 01709 813034

www.rotherham.gov.uk/sls

Dee Reid

Story illustrated **Andrew Painter**

Heinemann

Before Reading

Find out about

• All the mad things football fans get up to

Tricky words

• watch
• sheep
• singing
• England
• buy
• Wayne Rooney
• hair

Introduce these tricky words and help the reader when they come across them later!

Text starter

Are you a football fan? Are you football mad? Some people are so mad about football they do crazy things.

Mad Football Fans!

Lots of people like to watch football.

Lots of people like to play
football.
They are football fans.
Lots of football fans are
football mad.

Football fans like to watch football.
They like to play football.
They live for football.

Football fans go mad for football.

A fan made a CD of sheep singing. They were singing for the England team!

Football fans can buy a doll. The doll looks like Wayne Rooney.

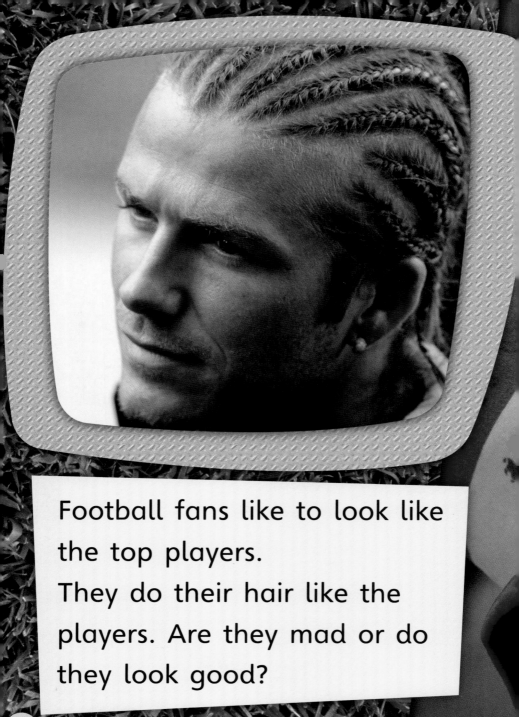

Football fans like to look like the top players.
They do their hair like the players. Are they mad or do they look good?

Football fans buy lots of football things.
Are they mad or do they look good?

Have you ever been to a football match?

Are you a football fan?
Do you go mad for football?

Quiz

Text Detective

- What mad things do football fans do?
- Are you a fan of anything?

Word Detective

- **Phonic Focus:** Blending three phonemes

  Page 6: Can you sound out 'fan'?
- Page 4: Can you find a word that means 'crazy'?
- Page 7: Why do the words 'Wayne Rooney' start with capital letters?

Super Speller

Read these words:

play looks top

Now try to spell them!

HA! HA! HA!

Q Why are footballers never invited to dinner?

A They're always dribbling!

Before Reading

In this story

 Big Bad Bill

 Big kids

 Little kids

 Introduce these tricky words and help the reader when they come across them later!

Tricky words

- playing
- football
- thing
- policeman
- goal
- really

Story starter

Big Bad Bill was big and bad. He loved to do bad things. One day, Big Bad Bill went to the park to find a bad thing to do. He saw some big kids playing football with some little kids.

Big Bad Bill and the Football

Bill was big.

Bill was bad.

"I am big bad Bill," said Bill.

Big Bad Bill went in the park. "I see some big kids and some little kids playing football," said Bill.
"What bad thing can I do?"

"I see a bad thing I can do," said Bill. "I can kick the football far away."

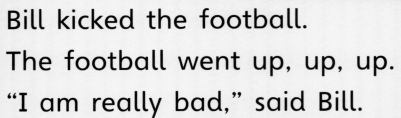

Bill kicked the football.
The football went up, up, up.
"I am really bad," said Bill.

The football went far away.

The football hit a big tree.

It hit a little tree.

The football hit a bin.

It hit a policeman.

The football went in the big kids' goal!

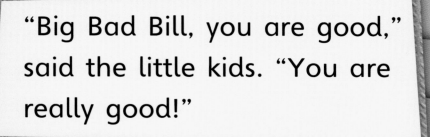

"Big Bad Bill, you are good," said the little kids. "You are really good!"

"You are Big Good Bill!" said
the little kids.

Quiz

Text Detective

- What did the football hit?
- Why did the little kids think Big Bad Bill was really good?

Word Detective

- **Phonic Focus:** Blending three phonemes

  Page 17: Can you sound out 'hit'?
- Page 13: How many words beginning with the phoneme 'b' are there on this page?
- Page 16: Find a word that means the opposite of 'down'.

Super Speller

Read these words:

some   kick   away

Now try to spell them!

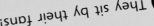

HA! HA! HA!

Q How do footballers keep cool?

A They sit by their fans!

24